## Fact Finders

Great Inventions

# THE TELEPHONE

by Marc Tyler Nobleman

Consultant:
Greg Russell
Telecommunications History Professional
Telephonymuseum.com

Capstone
press

Mankato, Minnesota

Fact Finders is published by Capstone Press,
151 Good Counsel Drive, P.O. Box 669, Mankato, Minnesota 56002.
www.capstonepress.com

*Library of Congress Cataloging-in-Publication Data*
Nobleman, Marc Tyler.
   The telephone / Marc Tyler Nobleman.
   p. cm.—(Fact finders. Great inventions)
   Includes bibliographical references (p. 31) and index.
   Contents: The first words—Before the telephone—Inventors—How a telephone
works—The telephone becomes popular—Telephones today.
   ISBN 0-7368-2218-6 (hardcover)
   ISBN 0-7368-4543-7 (paperback)
   1. Telephone—Juvenile literature. [1. Telephone.] I. Title. II. Series.
TK6165 .N63  2004
621.385—dc21                                                        2002156504

**Editorial Credits**
Roberta Schmidt, editor; Juliette Peters, series designer and illustrator; Alta Schaffer,
    photo researcher; Eric Kudalis, product planning editor

**Photo Credits**
Classic PIO Partners, cover, 26 (all), 27 (left)
Comstock, 16–17
Corbis, 4–5; Bettmann, 8, 9, 12–13; Underwood & Underwood, 14
Hulton/Archive Photos by Getty Images, 11, 15, 21, 22–23
Image Library, 1, 27 (middle, right)
North Wind Picture Archives, 6–7
Stockbyte, 24–25

1 2 3 4 5 6 08 07 06 05 04 03

# Table of Contents

# Chapter 1

# The First Words

"Mr. Watson, come here. I want to see you." Alexander Graham Bell said these words to Thomas Watson on March 10, 1876. Bell and Watson were in different rooms at the time. Bell wanted Watson to help him. He had spilled a chemical on his clothes.

Watson ran to Bell to tell him the good news. Watson had heard Bell's voice through their machine. Bell's words were the first words ever heard through a telephone.

That same day, Bell wrote a letter to his father. Bell told him the telephone

In the 1920s, a movie was made about Bell's 1876 invention.

was a great success. He said people would one day be able to talk to each other without leaving their homes.

# Chapter 2

# Before the Telephone

Before the telephone, most people talked to each other in person. They went to their friends' houses to talk to them. They walked, rode a horse, or traveled in a stagecoach to visit them.

People wrote letters to people who lived far away. Mail traveled slowly in the 1800s. A letter could take months to get to a person. Letters also cost a great deal of money to send.

In the mid-1800s, Samuel Morse invented a message-sending machine. This machine was called the telegraph.

In 1860, people had to pay $5 to send a letter. Today, that price would equal $90.

From April 1860 to November 1861, the Pony Express delivered mail and news to the western United States.

Messages were sent using a system of dots and dashes called Morse code. One message at a time was tapped out in Morse code on the machine. The machine sent the message through wires to another machine. This machine tapped the Morse code message onto paper.

Telegraphs helped people talk to each other over long distances. But telegraphs had some problems. People did not have telegraphs in their homes. They had to go to telegraph offices. Most people did not know Morse code. Telegraph operators had to send and read the messages.

| Morse Code | |
|---|---|
| A | . – |
| B | – . . . |
| C | – . – . |
| 1 | . – – – – |
| 2 | . . – – – |
| 3 | . . . – – |

Samuel Morse's telegraph used dots and dashes to send messages.

People went to offices to ask an operator to
send and receive their telegraph messages.

Telegraphs could send only one message at a
time. They sometimes did not work over very
long distances. People still needed a better way
to talk with friends and family.

# Chapter 3

# Inventors

The telephone was not invented by one person. Scientists in Great Britain, France, and Germany had ideas that led to the first telephone.

## Michael Faraday

In 1831, Michael Faraday worked with electricity. He was able to make electricity with a wire and a magnet. His work was later used by many inventors. People used electricity to develop many machines, including the telephone.

Michael Faraday was a British scientist.

## Charles Bourseul

In 1854, French scientist Charles Bourseul was studying sound. He knew that sound is made by vibrations. He believed machines could send and receive these vibrations. In this way, sound could be sent through wires over great distances. Bourseul's ideas encouraged many other inventors to work with sound and electricity.

## Johann Philipp Reis

In the early 1860s, Johann Philipp Reis sent sound over a distance. He built a machine that changed sound into electricity. He sent the electricity through a wire. The electricity was changed back into sound at the other end of the wire. Reis called his machine a telephone. But his invention could send only noise, not the human voice.

Johann Philipp Reis
was a German scientist.

The word "telephone"
comes from Greek
words that mean "far"
and "sound."

## Alexander Graham Bell

In 1876, Alexander Graham Bell made
the first telephone that worked with the
human voice. Bell was born in Scotland in
1847. He moved to America in the 1870s.
He was interested in sound and speech.

At first, Bell did not plan to invent
a telephone. He was trying to improve
the telegraph. Bell wanted to send more
than one message through a wire at a
time. He also wanted to send more than

Bell's first telephone had two parts. One part sent the sound. The other part received
the sound.

At one time, Alexander Graham Bell called his invention the "speaking telegraph."

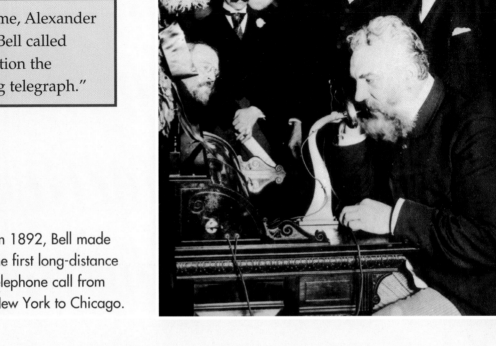

In 1892, Bell made the first long-distance telephone call from New York to Chicago.

Morse code messages. He wanted to send the human voice through the wires.

Bell built and tested machines for many years. On March 10, 1876, his machine worked. It sent Bell's voice through wires to another room. Bell and Watson kept working on the telephone. Seven months later, they talked to each other from two different towns.

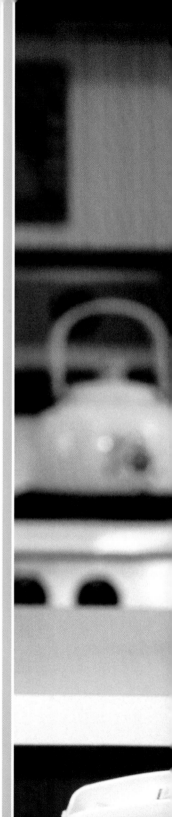

# Chapter 4

# How a Telephone Works

Telephones are electrical machines. They work by sending and receiving electrical signals.

A telephone changes a person's voice into electrical signals. These electrical signals then are sent through a wire. The wire carries the signals to another telephone. This telephone turns the electrical signals back into the person's voice.

A telephone changes a person's voice into electrical signals.

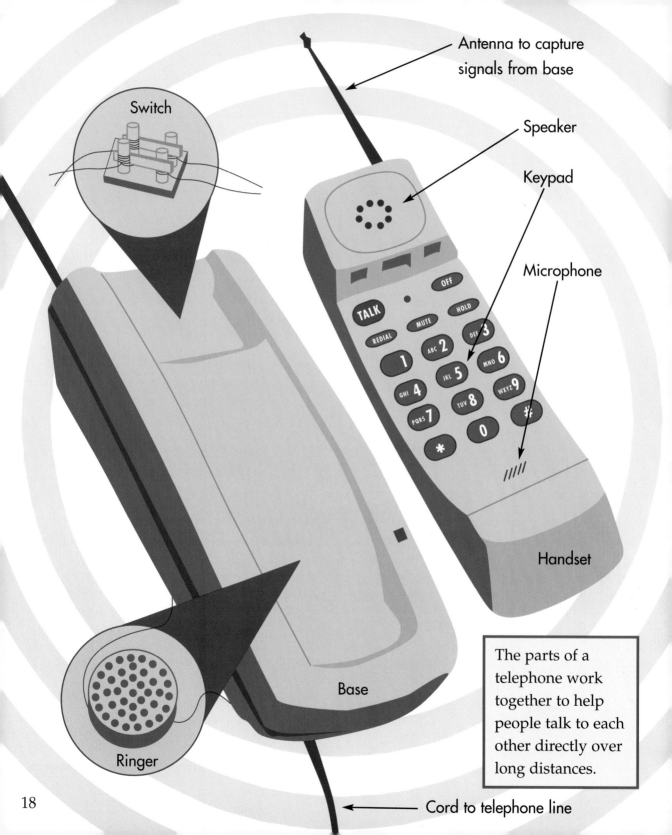

Antenna to capture signals from base

Speaker

Keypad

Microphone

Switch

TALK

OFF

MUTE

HOLD

REDIAL

DEF 3

ABC 2

1

JKL 5

MNO 6

GHI 4

WXYZ 9

TUV 8

PQRS 7

#

*

0

Handset

Base

Ringer

The parts of a telephone work together to help people talk to each other directly over long distances.

Cord to telephone line

Every telephone has a ringer, a microphone, a speaker, a switch, and a keypad. The ringer makes noise when someone is calling.

The microphone and the speaker are in the handset. The handset is the part a person holds. A person speaks into the microphone. The microphone changes sounds into electrical signals. A person puts the speaker by his or her ear. The speaker turns electrical signals into sounds.

A switch connects a telephone to a large system of telephones. A person cannot make a phone call if the switch is off. When the switch is on, the person hears a dial tone.

The buttons on the telephone are part of the keypad. A person presses the numbers to call another phone.

# Chapter 5

# The Telephone Becomes Popular

People were very interested in Bell's invention. Within one year, telephones were being used in many homes.

The number of phones in use grew quickly. In 1877, the Bell Telephone Company installed 230 telephones in the United States. By 1881, more than 47,900 telephones were in use. By 1915, the number was more than 10 million.

Telephones became very popular. They let people talk to each other directly.

In 1878, the first telephone exchange was set up in Connecticut. An exchange connects telephones. In the early years of telephones, operators worked at the exchanges. The operator sat in front of a switchboard. When people made a call, they talked to the operator first. The operator connected their phone to the other person's phone. Later, machines were built to work the exchanges.

Telephone operators connected phones through a switchboard.

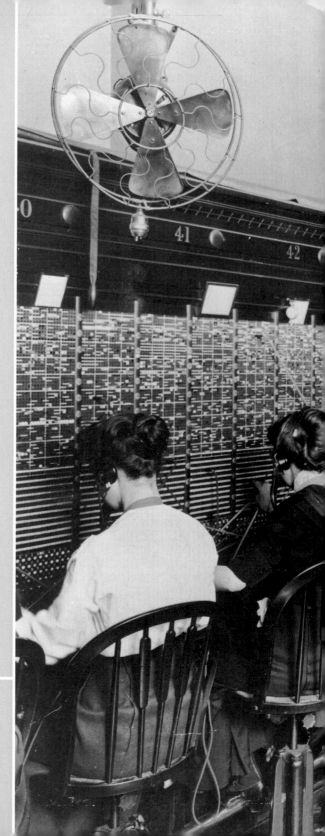

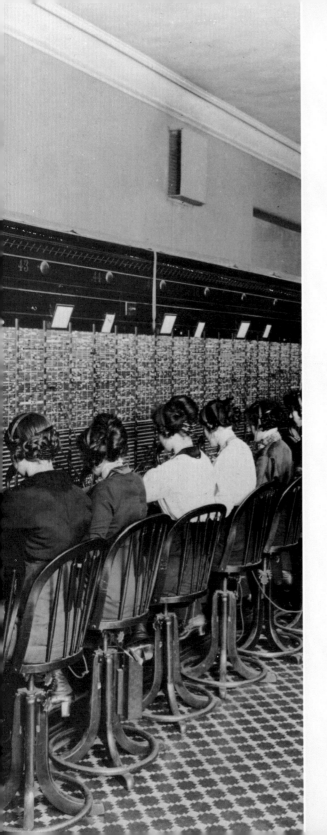

Rutherford B. Hayes was the first U.S. president to have telephone service. Telephones were installed in the White House in 1877.

For several years, telephones only worked over a short distance. Then long-distance telephone service developed in the late 1800s. The east and west coasts of the United States were connected by telephone in 1915.

In 1927, the first call was made across the Atlantic Ocean. The call connected people in New York City and London, England.

# Chapter 6

# Telephones Today

Today, many types of telephones are available. Most phones have different features and are easy to use.

Cordless phones send radio waves between the handset and the base. Electrical signals are carried on the radio waves rather than in a cord.

Cellular phones do not have cords or wires. They also are not connected to a telephone line. Cellular phones change voices into signals. These signals are carried on radio waves.

Cellular phones send messages over radio waves.

The radio waves travel to the nearest cell tower. From there, the radio wave is sent to another phone, and the signals are changed back into a voice.

Today, about 1 billion people worldwide use cellular phones.

## Telephone Services

Today's telephones can have many different services. With redial, a caller can retry a long phone number by pressing only one button. Call waiting

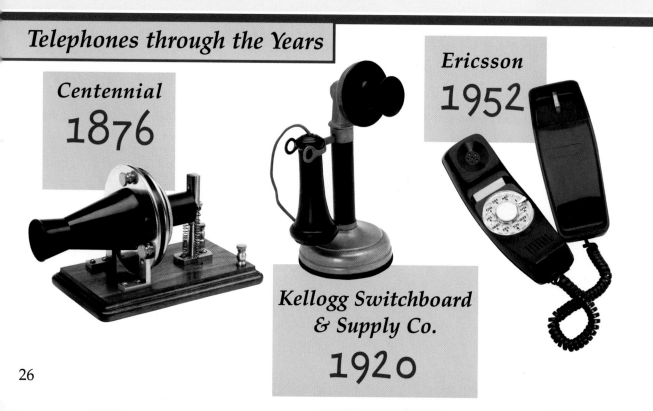

*Telephones through the Years*

*Centennial*
**1876**

*Ericsson*
**1952**

*Kellogg Switchboard & Supply Co.*
**1920**

lets a person receive other calls when the phone is in use. Caller ID allows a person to see the telephone number of a caller before answering. Some cellular phones let people write messages and send pictures over the phone.

Today, telephones are a very important part of everyday life. They help people keep in touch with their jobs, friends, and families.

GTE
1956

cordless from
1980s

cellular
today

# Fast Facts

- Before the telephone, people sent messages to each other through **letters** or **telegraphs**.

- **Johann Philipp Reis** built a telephone in the early 1860s. His telephone could only send noise, not the human voice.

- In 1876, **Alexander Graham Bell** made the first successful telephone that could send and receive the human voice.

- Bell formed the **Bell Telephone Company** in 1877. The company was later renamed **AT&T**.

- **Long-distance telephone service** developed in the late 1800s.

- The **first phone call** across the Atlantic Ocean was made in 1927. The call lasted 3 minutes and cost $75.

# Hands On:

## Make a Telephone

Children played with string telephones before the telephone was invented. You can make your own string telephone.

### What You Need
a sewing needle
2 large paper cups
100 feet (30 meters) of kite string
a friend

### What You Do
1. Use the sewing needle to punch a tiny hole in the center of the bottom of each cup.
2. Thread each end of the string through each hole. Tie a knot in the string to keep it from pulling out of the hole.
3. Take one cup. Give the other cup to your friend. Walk away from each other until the string is tight.
4. Take turns talking into your cups. While one person talks, the other person should hold the cup up to his or her ear.

The string works just like the wire in a real telephone. It carries the sound of the person's voice from the one cup to the other.

# Glossary

**exchange** (eks-CHAYNJ)—a system that connects many telephones

**experiment** (ek-SPER-uh-ment)—a scientific test; people do experiments to try something new.

**handset** (HAND-set)—the part of a telephone that a person holds

**install** (in-STAWL)—to put in

**invention** (in-VEN-shuhn)—a new thing

**inventor** (in-VEN-tuhr)—a person who makes something new

**receiver** (ri-SEE-vur)—a part in a telephone that changes an electric current back into a voice

**switchboard** (SWICH-bord)—the control center for connecting the lines of a telephone system

# Internet Sites

Do you want to find out more about the telephone?
Let FactHound, our fact-finding hound dog, do the research for you.

Here's how:
1) Visit *http://www.facthound.com*
2) Type in the **Book ID** number:
   **0736822186**
3) Click on **FETCH IT**.

FactHound will fetch Internet sites picked by our editors just for you!

# Read More

**Alphin, Elaine Marie.** *Telephones.* Household History. Minneapolis: Carolrhoda Books, 2001.

**Gearhart, Sarah.** *The Telephone.* Turning Point Inventions. New York: Atheneum Books for Young Readers, 1999.

**Stille, Darlene R.** *Telephones.* Let's See. Minneapolis: Compass Point Books, 2002.

# Index